Daddy, Am I Beautiful?

Written by Michelle S. Lazurek

Illustrated by Apryl Stott

Pauline
BOOKS & MEDIA
Boston

Library of Congress Cataloging-in-Publication Data

Lazurek, Michelle S., author.
  Daddy, am I beautiful? / written by Michelle S. Lazurek ; illustrated by Apryl Stott.
    pages cm
  Audience: Ages 4-7
  ISBN 978-0-8198-1905-5 (pbk.) -- ISBN 0-8198-1905-0 (pbk.)
  1. Girls--Conduct of life--Juvenile literature. 2. Christian life--Juvenile literature. 3.
Conduct of life--Juvenile literature. I. Stott, Apryl, illustrator. II. Title.
  BV4551.3.L39 2015
  248.8'2--dc23
                              2015011418

The Scripture quotations contained herein are from the *New Revised Standard Version Bible: Catholic Edition*, copyright © 1989, 1993, Division of Christian Education of the National Council of the Churches of Christ in the United States of America. Used by permission. All rights reserved.

Design by Mary Joseph Peterson, FSP

Illustrations by Apryl Stott

Published by Pauline Books & Media, 50 Saint Pauls Avenue, Boston, MA 02130–3491

Printed in the U.S.A.

DAIB VSAUSAPEOILL6-3010048 1905-0

www.pauline.org

Pauline Books & Media is the publishing house of the Daughters of St. Paul, an international congregation of women religious serving the Church with the communications media.

1 2 3 4 5 6 7 8 9   20 19 18 17 16 15

"The LORD does not see as mortals see;

they look on the outward appearance,

but the LORD looks on the heart."

— *1 Samuel 16:7*

To Leah,

Your Father will always think you are beautiful.

Lovely Leah loved to play dress-up. She spent hours putting on her most beautiful princess gowns from her treasure chest and dancing around her room.

She went out to show Daddy, who was planting seeds in the garden, how she looked. Leah twirled herself around and turned her gown into a rainbow-colored blur.

"Daddy, am I beautiful?" she asked.

"Of course, Leah," Daddy said. "You're beautiful all the time and everywhere."

Leah ran back inside. She put on all her beaded
necklaces, three princess crowns, and her sparkly pink
shoes and went back to the garden.

"Daddy, am I *more* beautiful now?" she asked.

"You are as beautiful as you always have been,"
Daddy said. "You're beautiful all the time and
everywhere."

Just then, Leah spotted the large pile of dirt Daddy was digging in and decided to join him. As she helped Daddy dig holes and plant some seeds, the dirt stained her dress. The once beautiful rainbow gown was now an ugly brown mess.

"Oh no!" cried Leah, with tears welling up in her eyes. "I'm not beautiful anymore. . . "

"Leah, sweetie, you are the *most* beautiful now,"
Daddy said.

"Daddy, how can I be the most beautiful now?
I'm all dirty!"

Daddy put his arm around her, and looked into
Leah's eyes. Tears now slipped down her rosy cheeks.

"You're beautiful because you're helping," Daddy
said. "God makes you beautiful from the inside out.
God's love is what true beauty is all about."

"I don't understand, Daddy. My princess dress
is what makes me beautiful."

"It's not the dress or the crowns, Leah. *You* are
beautiful all the time and everywhere."

"I am?" sniffed Leah.

"Yes, you are," Daddy said. "Look at the seed in your hand. Do you think it's beautiful?"

"No," said Leah. "It's just a seed."

"The seed may not look like much, but it's still beautiful. Beauty is more than what we can see on the outside, Leah." Daddy pointed to the bright and colorful spring flowers growing outside the front window. "See those flowers that are blooming?"

"The purple ones are my favorite," giggled Leah.

"All those flowers started as little seeds. On the inside each seed has everything it needs to become the flower God made it to be. See here?" Daddy asked while pointing to the picture on the front of the seed packet.

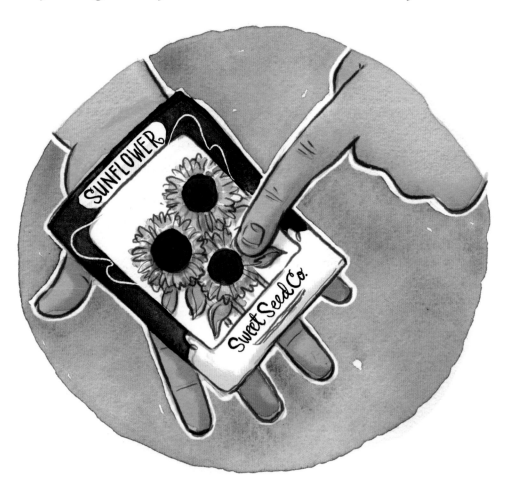

"Those flowers come from these seeds, Daddy?"
wondered Leah.

"Yes, sweetie, these seeds will become big,
yellow sunflowers."

"Wow, these seeds are amazing!" Leah exclaimed,
her eyes wide open.

"That's because God made them!" Daddy smiled. "But seeds don't grow on their own. God sends the sun and the rain to help them grow into what he created them to be. Each seed can become a flower. Then its inside beauty isn't hidden anymore. Everyone can see how beautiful it is."

"But I'm not a seed, Daddy. How will everyone see my inside beauty?" Leah wondered aloud.

"In the Bible, God teaches us that whenever we act the way he wants us to act—like when we forgive someone who has hurt us, or share what we have—other people can see the beauty inside us."

"Is *everyone* beautiful, Daddy?" asked Leah.

"Yes," said Daddy. "God made you, and me, and Mommy, and all people. God makes every one of us beautiful from the inside out. God's love is what true beauty is all about."

Leah thought for a moment. Her forehead wrinkled. Suddenly, her face beamed. She knew exactly what to do to make her inner beauty show. Leah ran upstairs and put all of her toys away. Daddy followed her and smiled.

"Daddy, am I beautiful?" she asked him.

"Absolutely!" Daddy said.

Then, she went into her brother's room and gave back his favorite airplane. She apologized for having taken it and gave him a big hug.

"Daddy, am I beautiful now?" she asked.

"Leah, you're beautiful. You could have green skin, or spaghetti and meatballs for hair, and you would still be beautiful all the time and everywhere. God makes you beautiful from the inside out. God's love is what true beauty is all about."

Lovely Leah took off her dirty princess dress and placed it in the hamper. She then carefully put her crowns and beaded necklaces away in her toy box.

"Leah, why did you put all of your dress-up clothes away? Don't you think they are beautiful anymore?" Daddy asked.

"Yes. But I don't need them to make *me* beautiful. I'm already beautiful because God made me that way. Right, Daddy?"

Daddy nodded. "Don't ever forget that, Leah. God made you beautiful, and you can show your beauty all the time and everywhere."

Leah turned and giggled. "Because we could have green skin or spaghetti and meatballs for hair. And we would still be beautiful, all the time and everywhere, Daddy!"

Leah began to twirl and dance around her room.
"God makes us beautiful from the inside out," she sang.
"God's love is what true beauty is all about."

For Grown-Ups

My three-year-old daughter paraded in front of her father one day and asked, "Daddy, am I beautiful?" In that moment, I realized that every girl—no matter her age—desires to know that she is beautiful. From their earliest years, girls are encouraged by media and society to believe that their worth comes from their outward appearance. In a world where we are told that image is everything, *Daddy, Am I Beautiful?* is intended to help parents and educators teach little girls the truth. The value of each person flows from the fact that we are created by God in his image. Beauty is God's gift to every one of us. Our beauty is both internal and external. We reveal it through our bodies, our words, our actions—in short, by every aspect of who we are.

This book

🌸 explores self-esteem from the perspective of a little girl;

🌸 roots a person's worth in God's unconditional love;

🌸 shows that the beauty God gives us shines through the things we do in accordance with God's love.

Through an entertaining story and engaging illustrations, *Daddy, Am I Beautiful?* aims to lead little girls to a lively self-acceptance and encourages them to embrace the fullness of their God-given beauty for the rest of their lives.

As you share this book with your little girl, let her know that: "God makes you beautiful from the inside out. God's love is what true beauty is all about."

Michelle S. Lazurek is a pastor's wife, mother, Bible teacher, author, and speaker who encourages ordinary people to become extraordinary disciples. Through the art of storytelling, Michelle writes books that inspire and teach children biblical values. In addition to *Daddy, Am I Beautiful?* Michelle has written a book for boys titled *Mommy, Am I Strong?* (Pauline Books & Media 2015). Learn more about Michelle at www.michellelazurek.com.

Apryl Stott loves to draw and paint. She studied illustration and design at Brigham Young University. As a freelance illustrator, she's drawn pictures for books, card games, postcards, stickers, posters, school books, and lots of magazines. This is her second book for Pauline Books & Media. You can find out more about her work at aprylstottdesign.com. She lives in Northern Nevada with her husband, two daughters, a snuggly cat, and five pet chickens.

Positively **Human** kids
Pauline

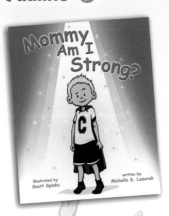

Who are the Daughters of St. Paul?

We are Catholic sisters.
Our mission is to be like
Saint Paul and tell everyone
about Jesus! There are so
many ways for people to
communicate with each
other. We want to use all of
them so everyone will know
how much God loves us. We
do this by printing books (you're
holding one!),
making radio shows,
singing, helping people at
our bookstores, using the
internet, and in many other
ways.

Visit our Web site at www.pauline.org